HANUKKAH

ACTIVITY BOOK
FOR KIDS

This Book
Belongs To:

_____

_____

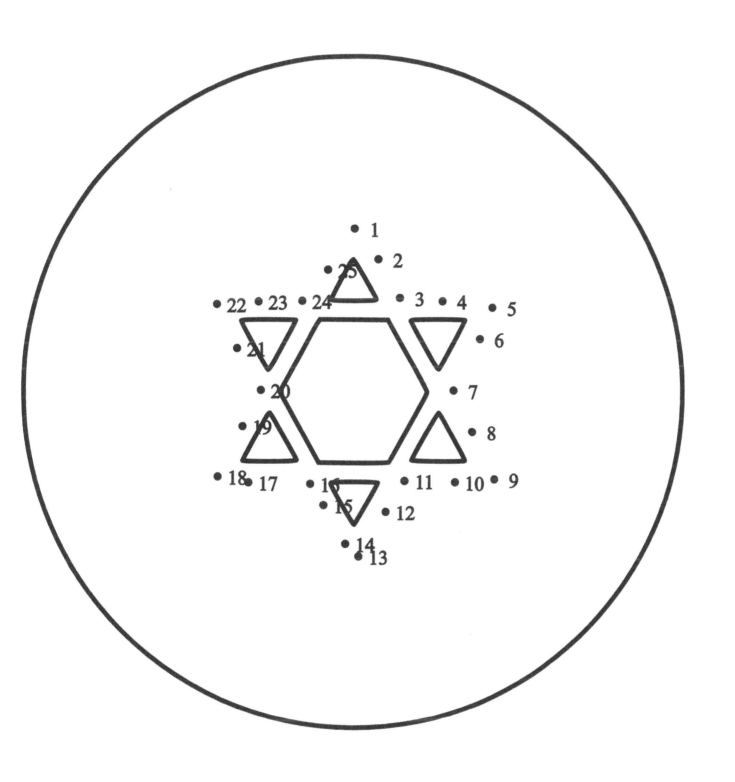

Help the menorah through the maze.

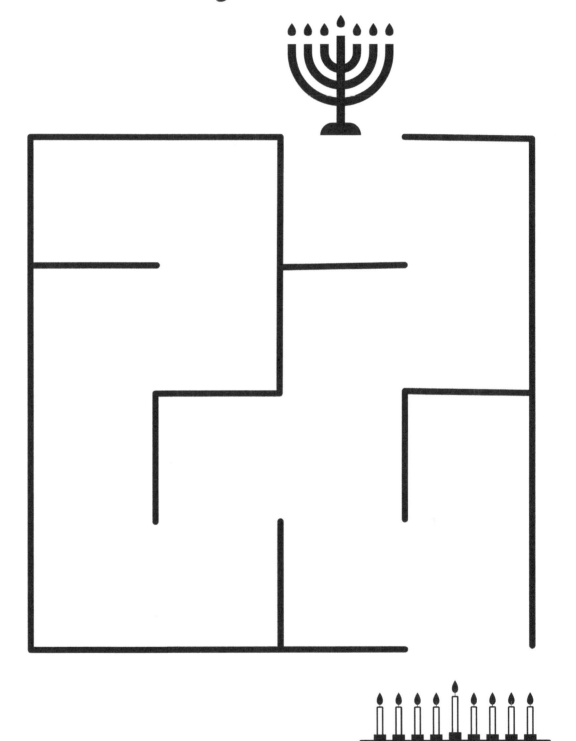

Word Search Circle The Below Words

N	I	Q	V	C	B	Y	R	M
Q	R	Q	A	N	B	A	U	W
K	T	X	H	B	D	R	A	T
Y	O	Y	C	N	E	A	C	B
W	W	S	E	T	Z	D	N	I
E	P	L	N	W	L	V	V	C
C	A	E	Y	C	X	M	A	L
C	C	S	E	L	D	N	A	C
B	L	E	S	S	I	N	G	S

Word List

blessings   calendar   candles   center

COUNT AND TRACE

Spot The Differences

Count And Trace

1

2

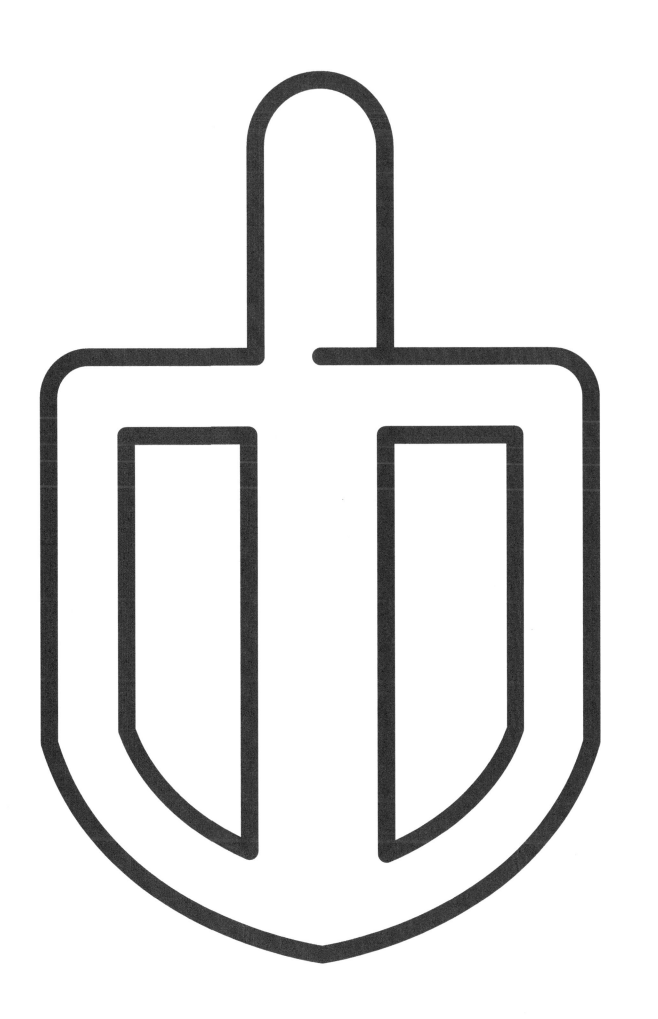

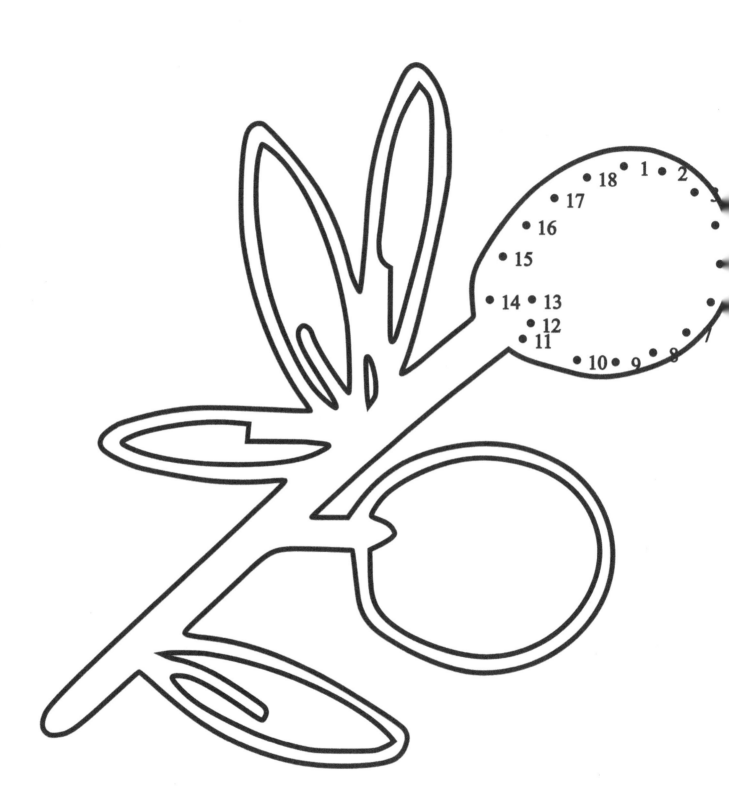

Help the book
through the maze.

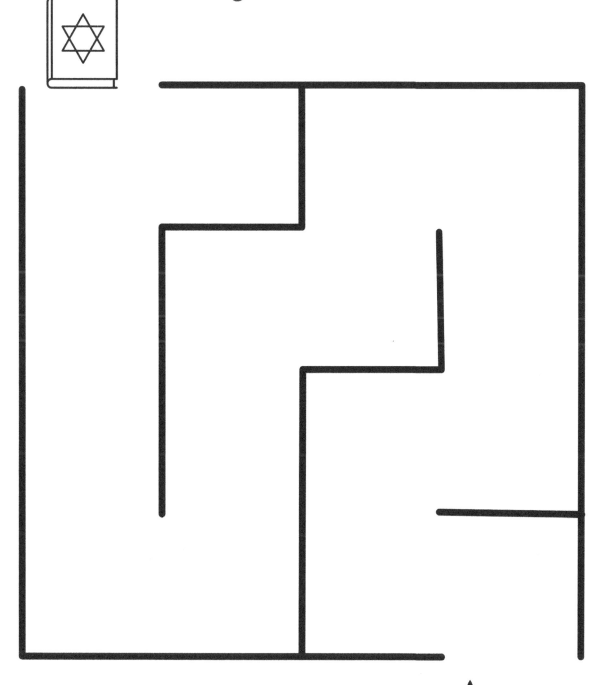

Word Search Circle The Below Words

V	O	V	L	B	N	I	Z	J
H	A	K	U	N	A	H	C	C
O	Q	X	L	E	Q	C	X	H
F	B	X	K	N	H	F	K	I
B	L	W	T	E	B	R	X	L
E	J	M	E	T	B	V	F	D
P	P	R	Z	T	N	Z	M	R
C	H	O	C	O	L	A	T	E
K	K	H	B	A	K	B	Z	N

Word List

chanukah   cheer   children   chocolate

COUNT AND TRACE

12

12 12 12 12 12 12

12 12 12 12 12 12

12 12 12 12 12 12

12 12 12 12 12 12

Spot The Differences

Count And Trace

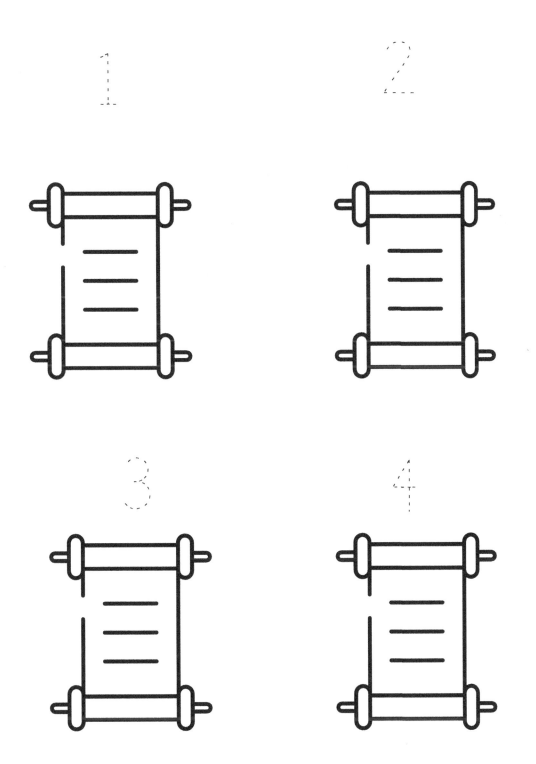

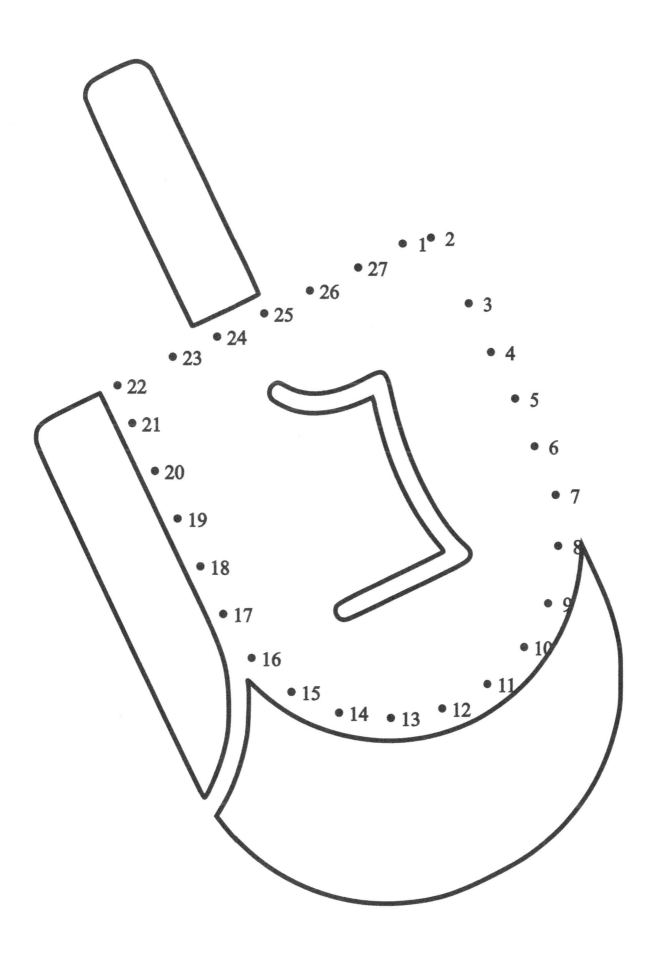

Help the present through the maze.

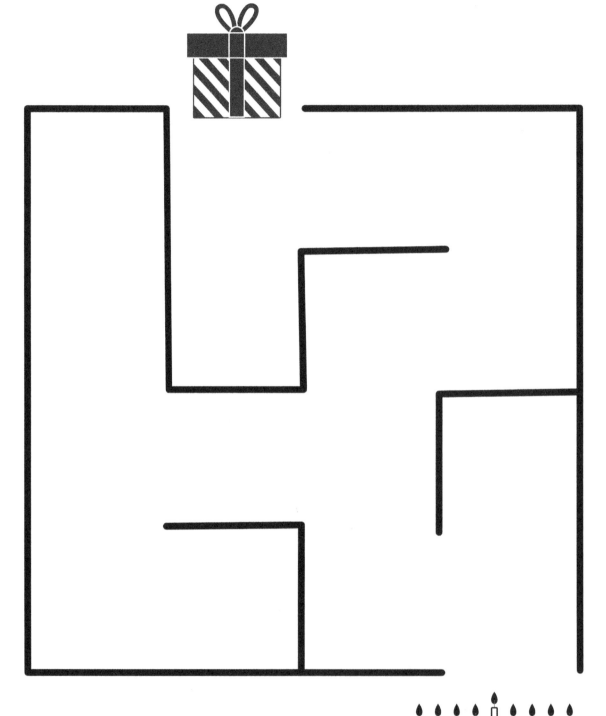

Word Search Circle The Below Words

C	O	M	M	U	N	I	T	Y
T	C	F	W	S	A	W	X	H
J	K	O	N	N	I	V	T	L
Y	Z	I	V	P	C	A	K	J
V	O	Q	R	E	B	F	L	W
C	V	U	V	B	N	T	G	U
T	I	I	A	A	Z	A	F	A
N	Q	S	Z	N	X	R	N	H
Y	W	C	B	I	N	N	H	T

Word List

coins   community covenant   sabbath

COUNT AND TRACE

Spot The Difference

Count And Trace

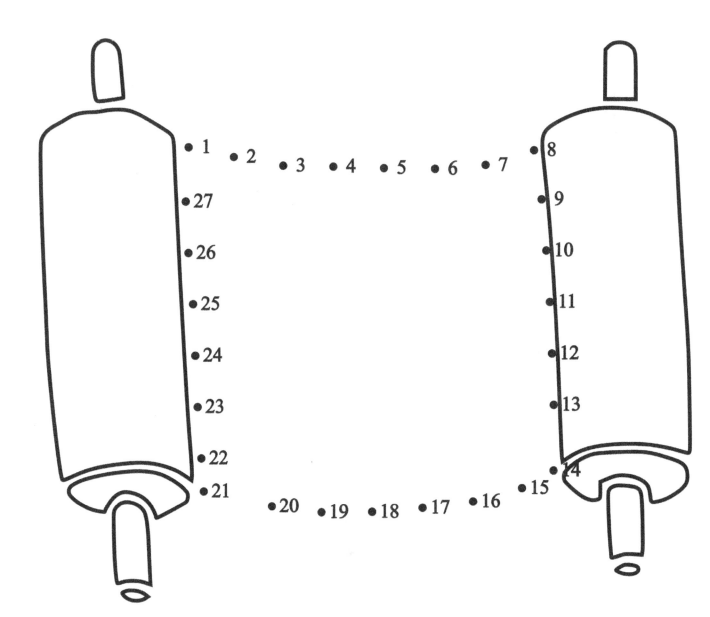

Help the cake through the maze.

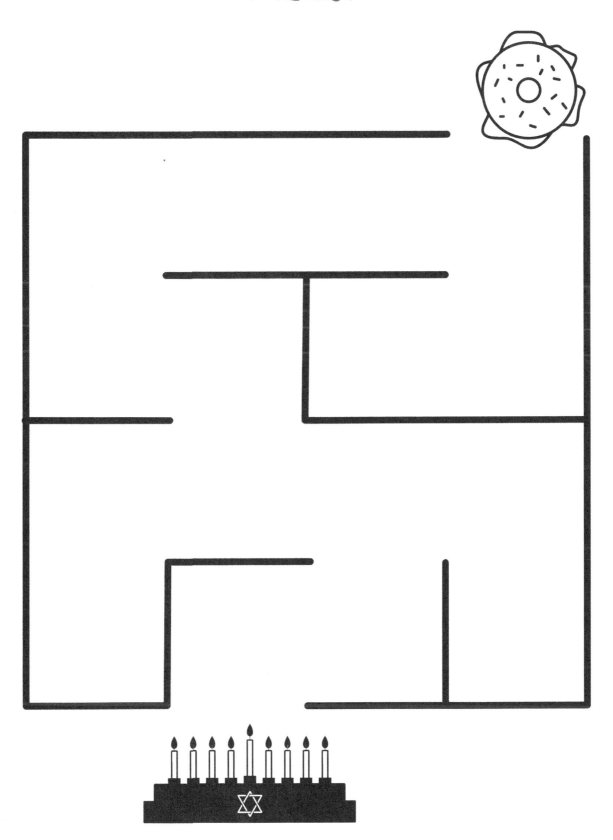

Word Search Circle The Below Words

L	L	E	D	I	E	R	D	R
K	W	Y	Y	A	P	U	E	U
B	V	I	R	R	R	B	A	G
S	S	T	V	I	M	I	D	F
L	V	L	H	E	A	Q	F	E
H	T	C	C	G	P	D	Z	E
W	O	E	E	U	I	I	S	C
G	D	G	H	K	B	E	S	N
K	V	L	M	L	M	V	V	S

Word List

dairy   december   dreidel   eight

COUNT AND TRACE

Spot The Difference

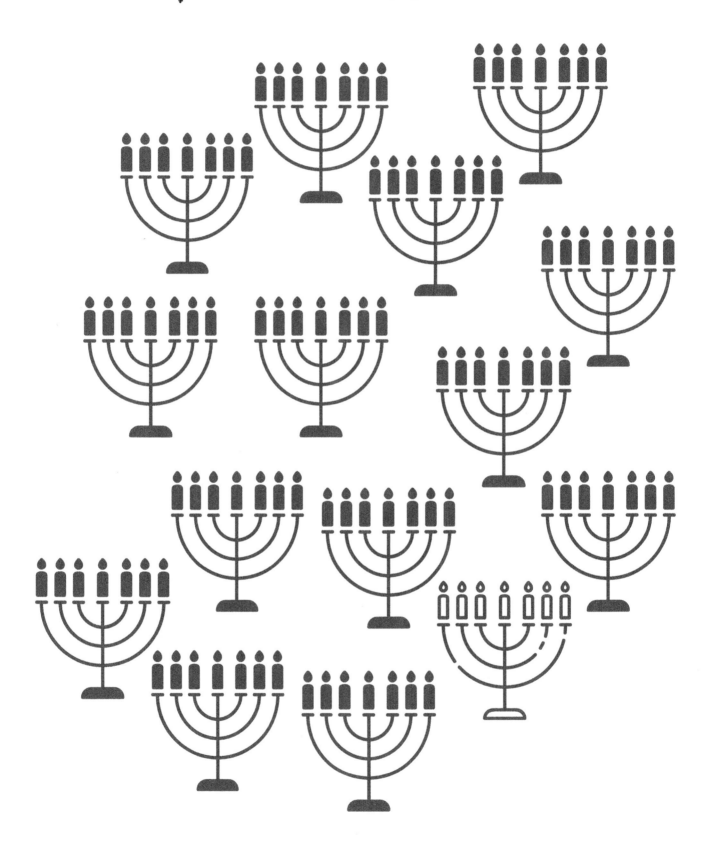

Count And Trace

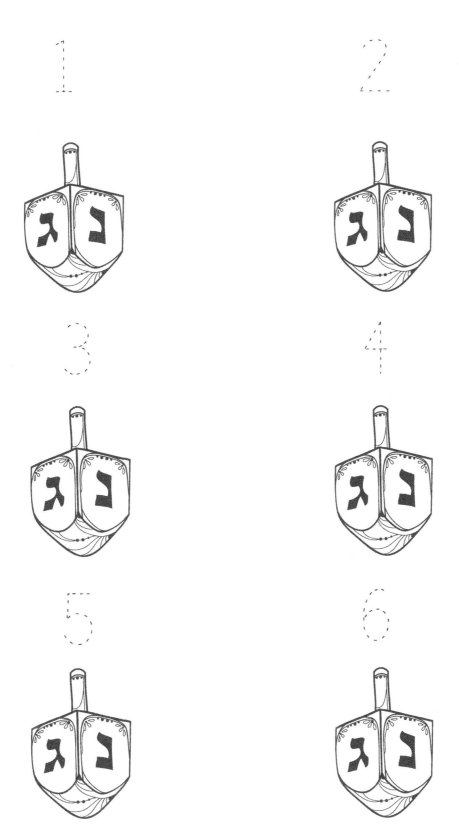

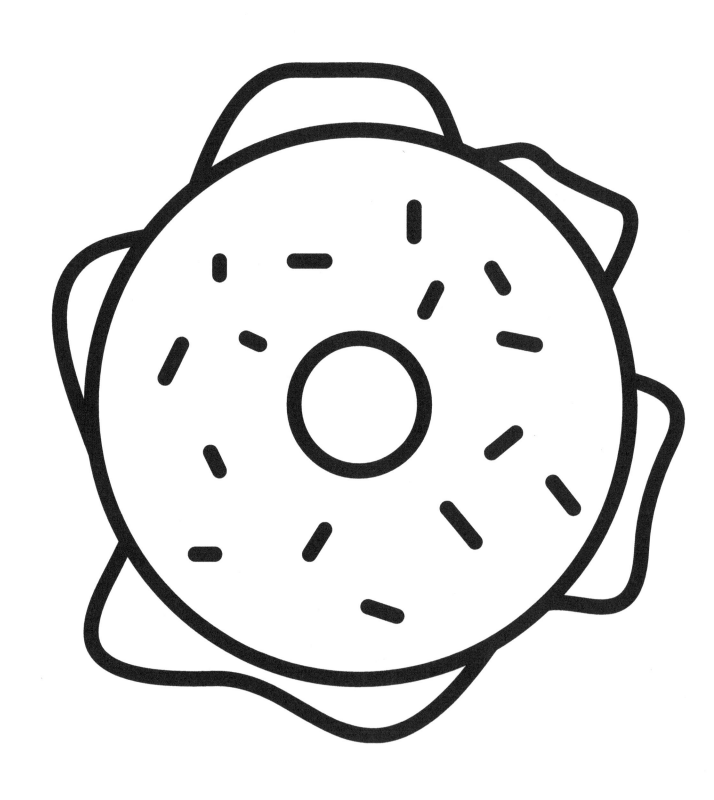

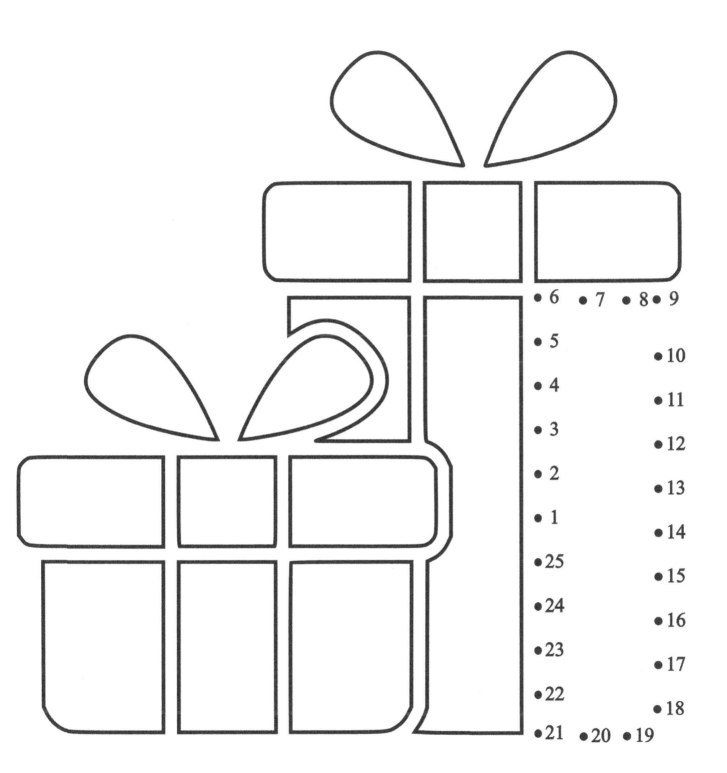

Help the star of david through the maze.

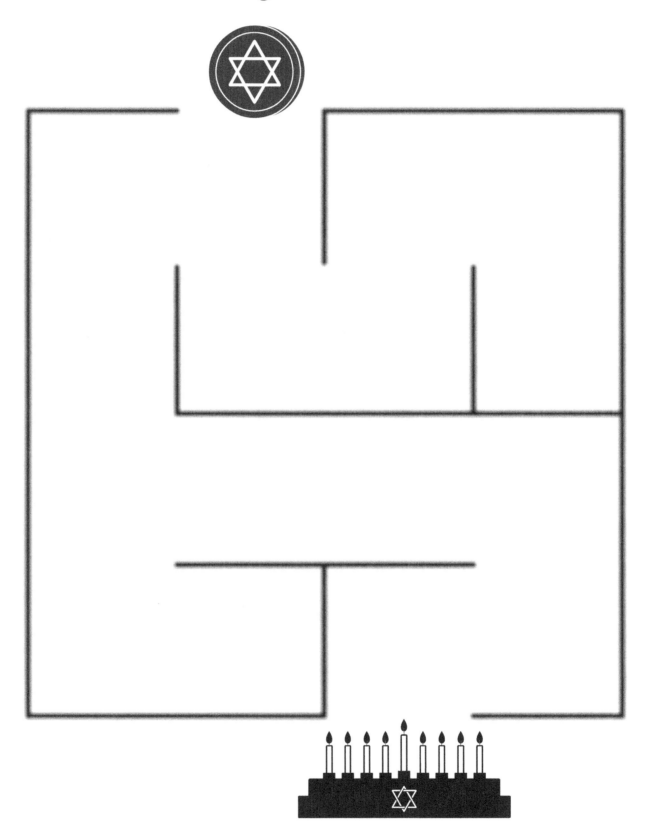

Word Search Circle The Below Words

N	O	J	N	R	C	T	F	L
I	N	C	A	M	L	B	P	F
Q	R	Y	J	J	J	S	Q	A
E	V	E	N	T	H	A	H	M
O	M	X	L	T	Z	T	N	I
W	N	H	C	K	I	G	X	L
S	F	A	W	A	W	K	P	Y
V	N	Q	F	Y	C	B	W	V
E	S	Z	A	K	T	I	Q	E

Word List

enact   event   faith   family

COUNT AND TRACE

Spot The Difference

Count And Trace

1

2

3

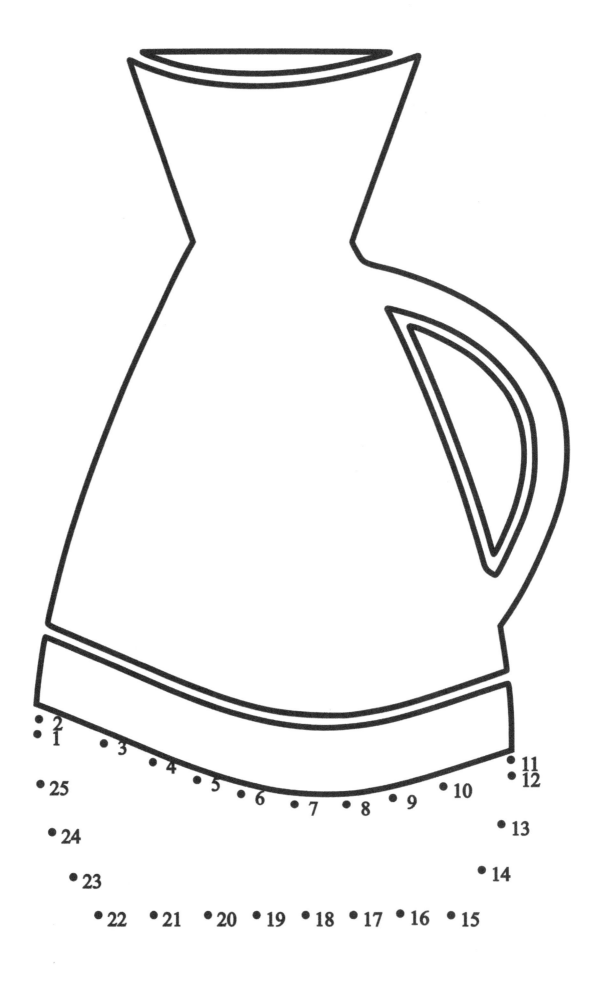

Help the cup through the maze.

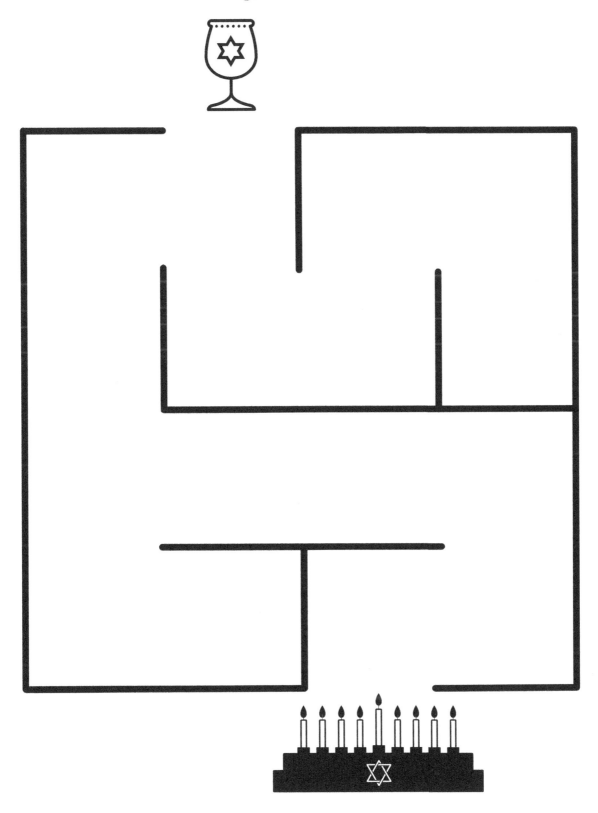

Word Search Circle The Below Words

X	I	S	E	M	A	G	F	M
N	L	L	O	Q	D	K	O	K
O	W	A	L	Q	C	N	C	L
I	K	U	V	L	N	X	U	M
M	W	K	T	I	P	H	S	F
M	D	M	Q	L	T	M	Q	X
D	O	O	F	I	F	S	E	Q
T	P	X	U	X	X	I	E	B
L	V	S	D	X	W	Y	N	F

Word List

festival   focus   food   games

COUNT AND TRACE

Spot The Difference

Count And Trace

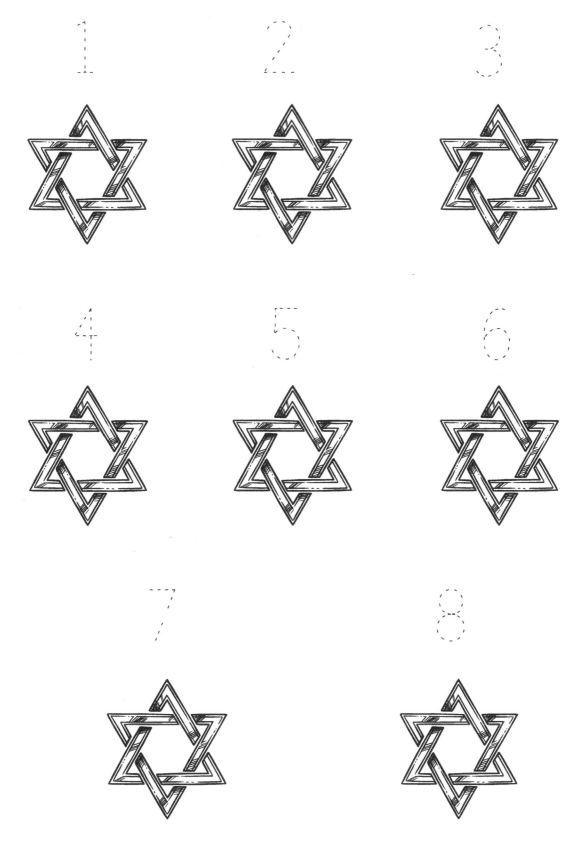

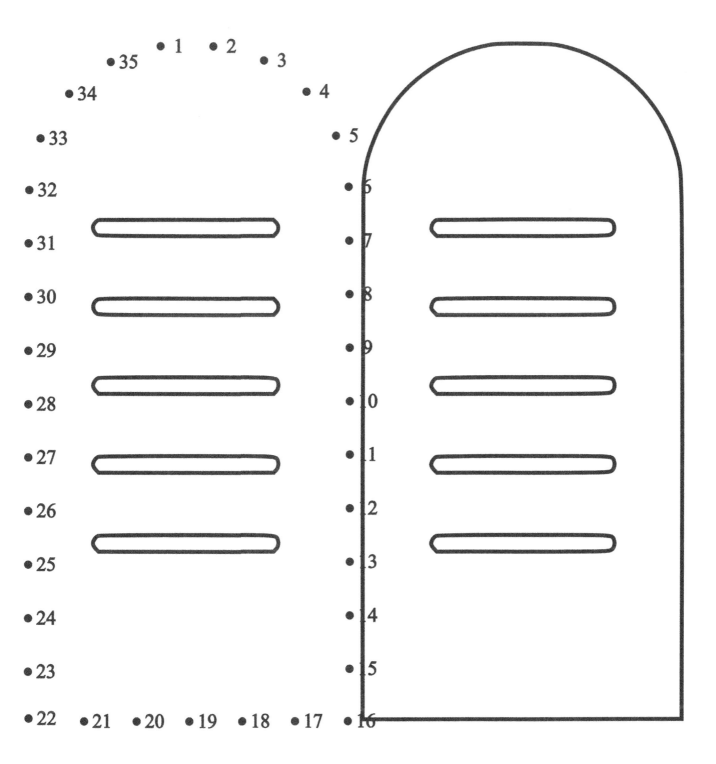

Help the candles through the maze.

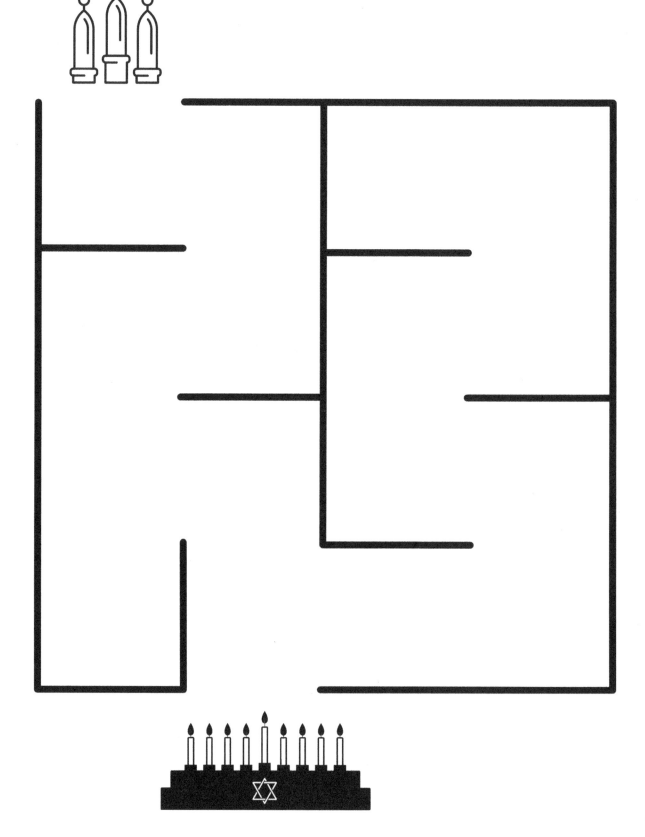

Word Search Circle The Below Words

J	A	R	S	G	S	Q	K	T
H	G	M	J	C	L	R	C	V
A	L	D	G	E	B	W	P	C
G	H	O	M	I	A	K	N	Q
E	E	I	A	P	F	I	N	V
L	G	W	H	L	N	T	O	M
T	I	Z	X	A	E	I	S	O
B	B	E	T	G	O	D	M	A
T	R	D	V	L	O	H	X	J

Word List

gelt   gifts   gimel   god

COUNT AND TRACE

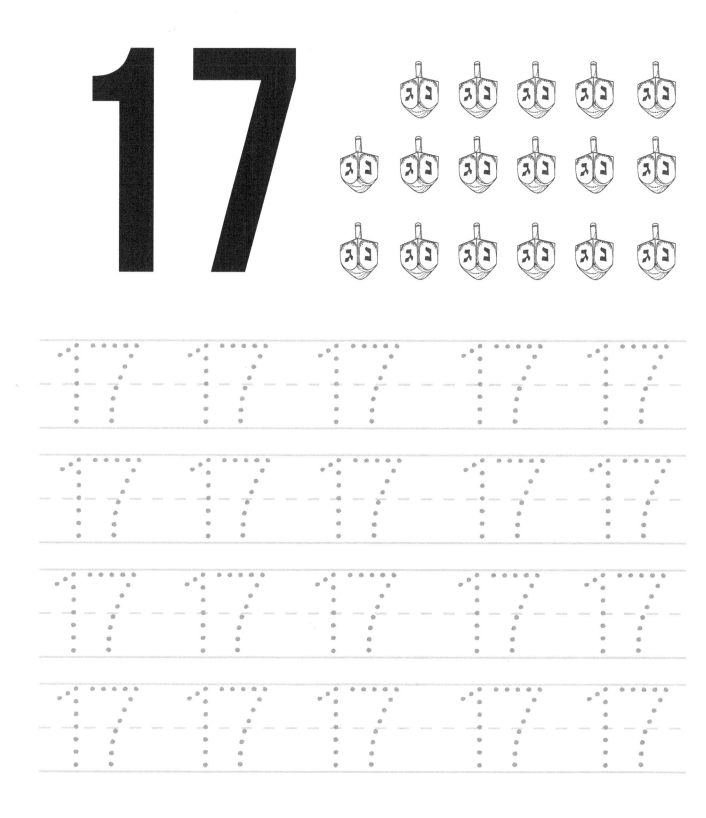

Spot The Difference

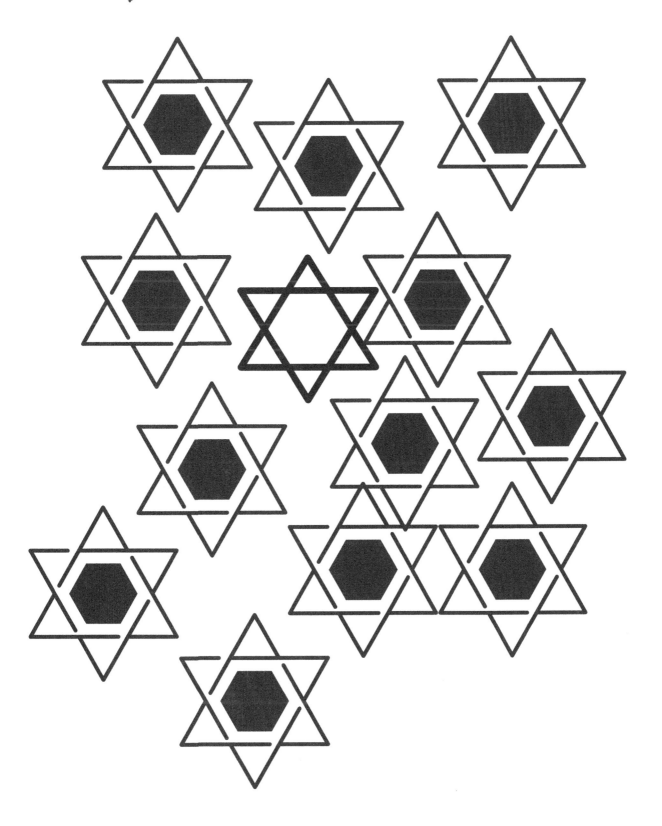

Count And Trace

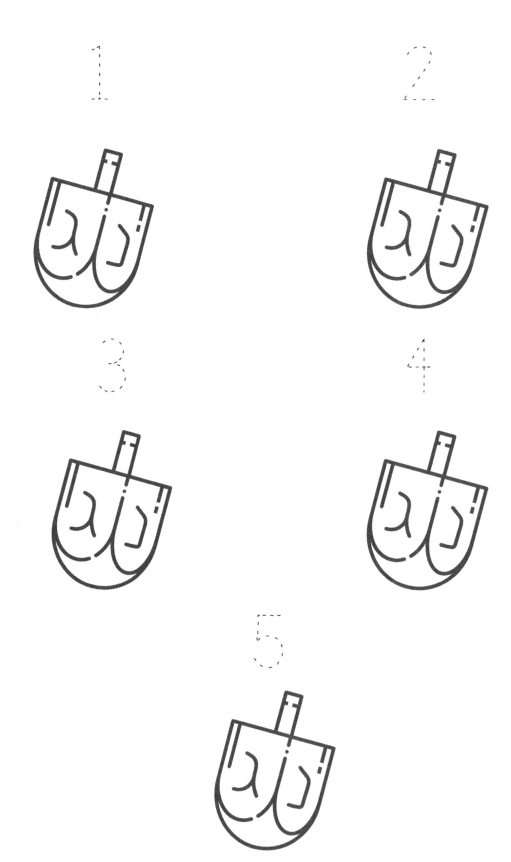

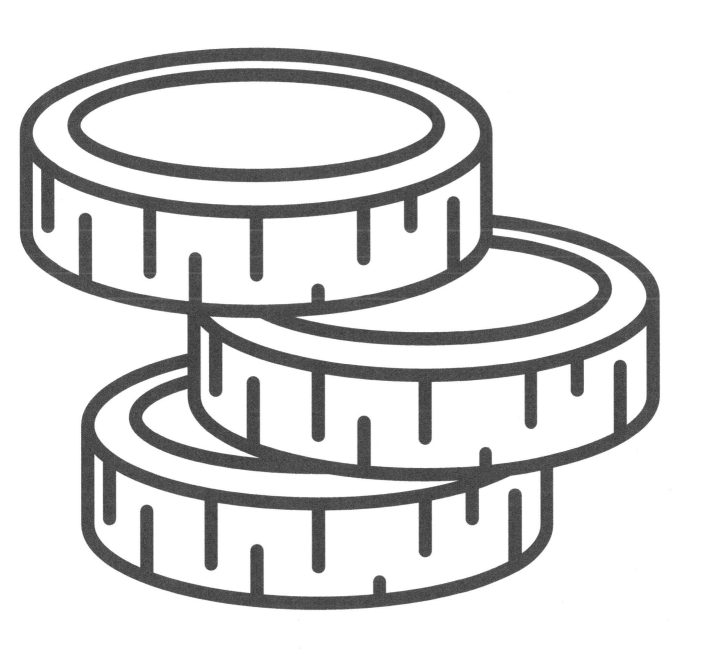

Help the dreidel through the maze.

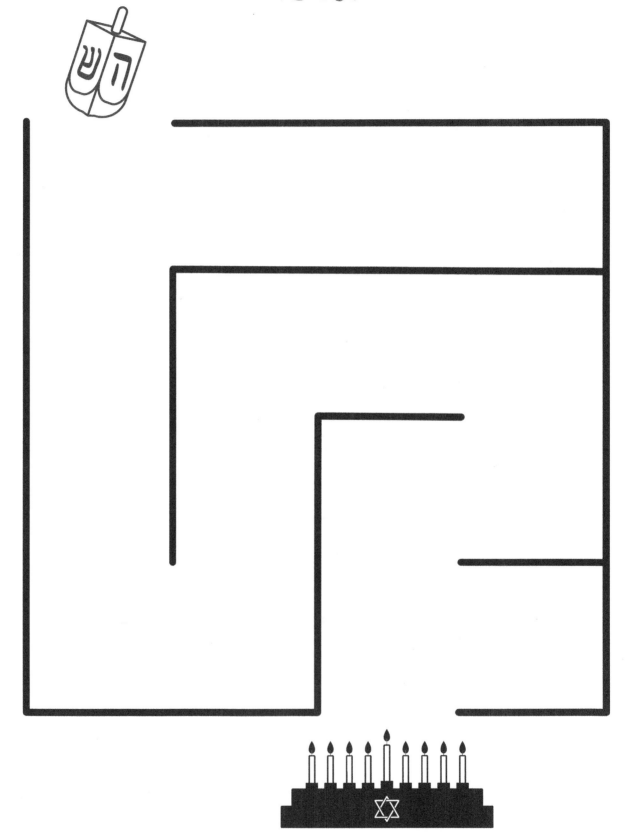

Word Search Circle The Below Words

C	I	A	X	G	K	W	S	E
I	W	Q	I	M	E	G	V	W
D	S	R	K	R	Y	H	E	J
U	C	R	B	U	A	W	W	J
Z	R	E	A	L	D	A	N	V
D	H	H	L	E	I	P	B	O
Y	O	E	A	K	L	X	Y	G
C	L	I	U	B	O	V	Y	B
T	S	V	E	X	H	M	Y	L

Word List

hallel   hebrew   holiday   israel

COUNT AND TRACE

18

Spot The Difference

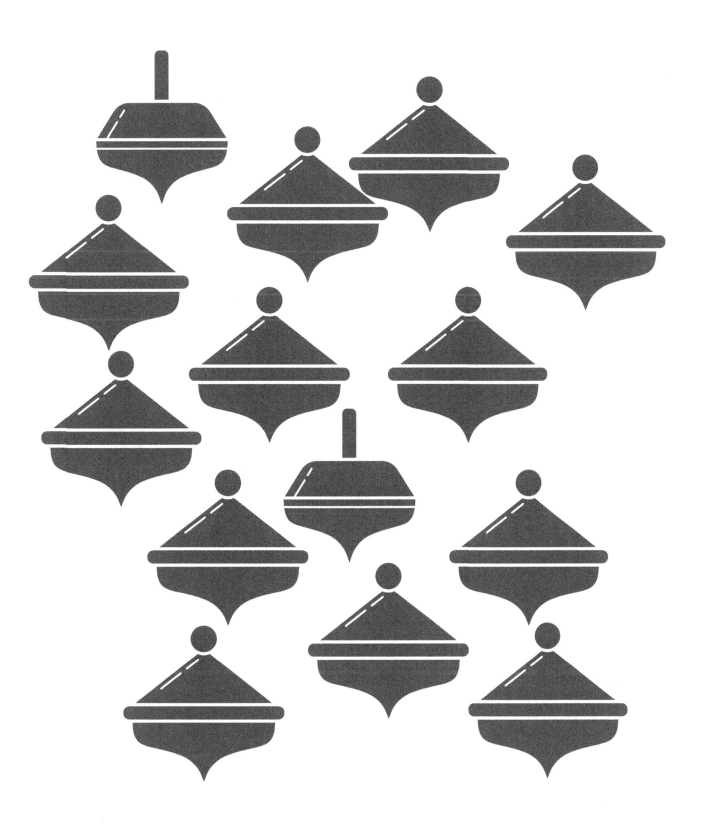

Count And Trace

1

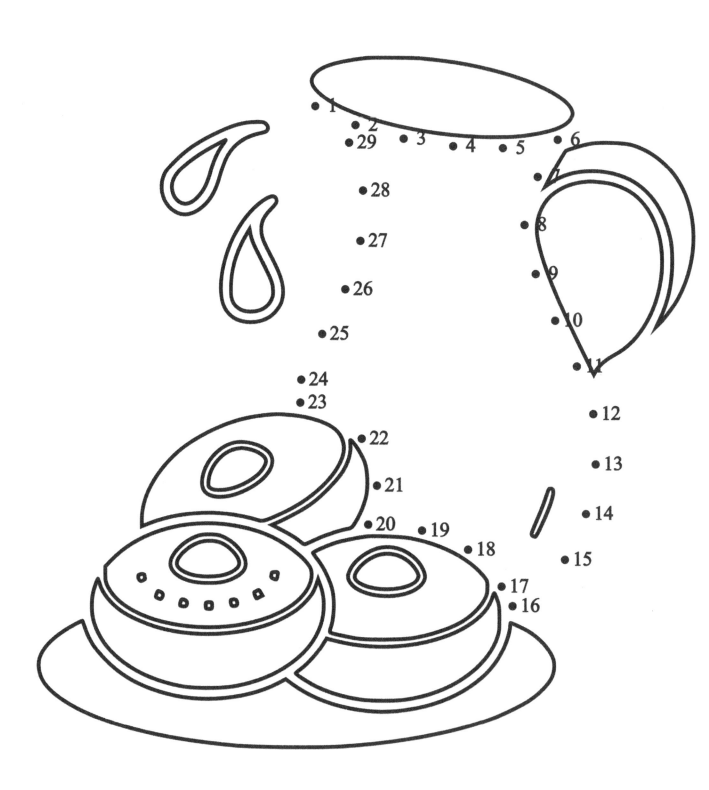

Help the gelt through the maze.

Word Search Circle The Below Words

H	P	W	L	K	Q	W	M	Z
X	J	E	W	I	S	H	V	L
L	V	R	U	N	O	S	D	P
Y	I	N	K	D	J	I	K	C
K	K	V	P	L	S	D	A	T
X	Q	V	I	E	H	L	F	J
J	H	Y	H	V	S	Q	F	X
M	Q	X	B	B	O	D	J	Z
V	E	L	S	I	K	T	M	I

Word List

jewish   kindle   kislev   livivot

COUNT AND TRACE

Spot The Differences

Count And Trace

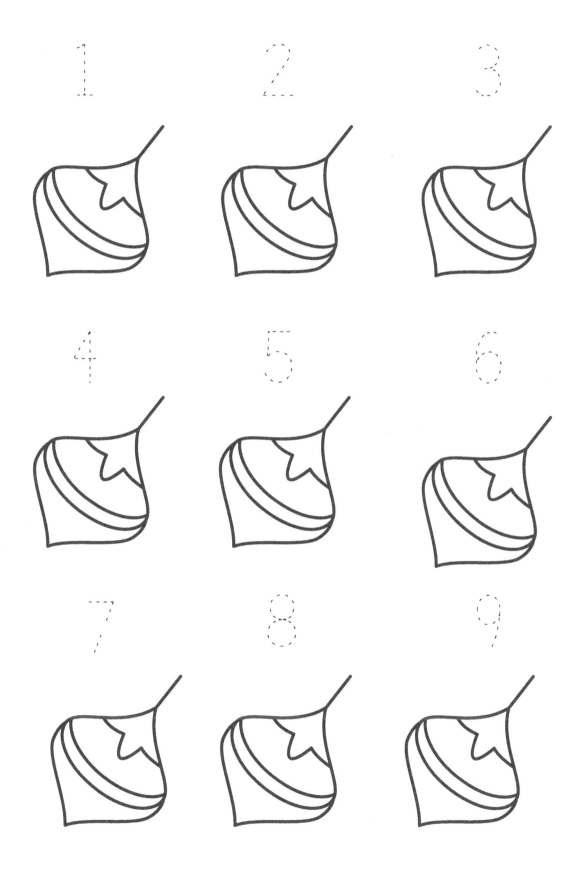

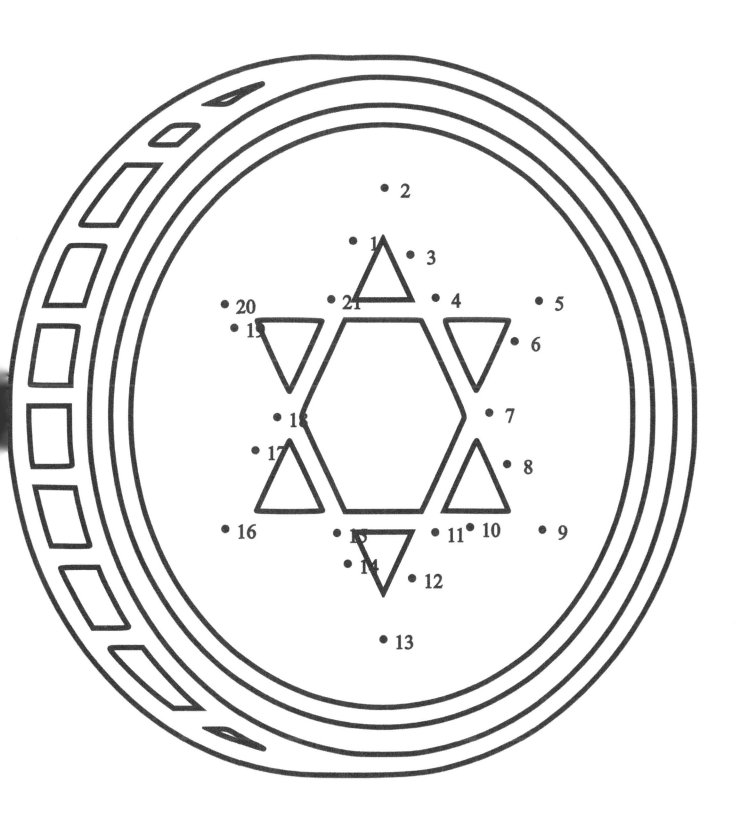

Help the ol through the maze.

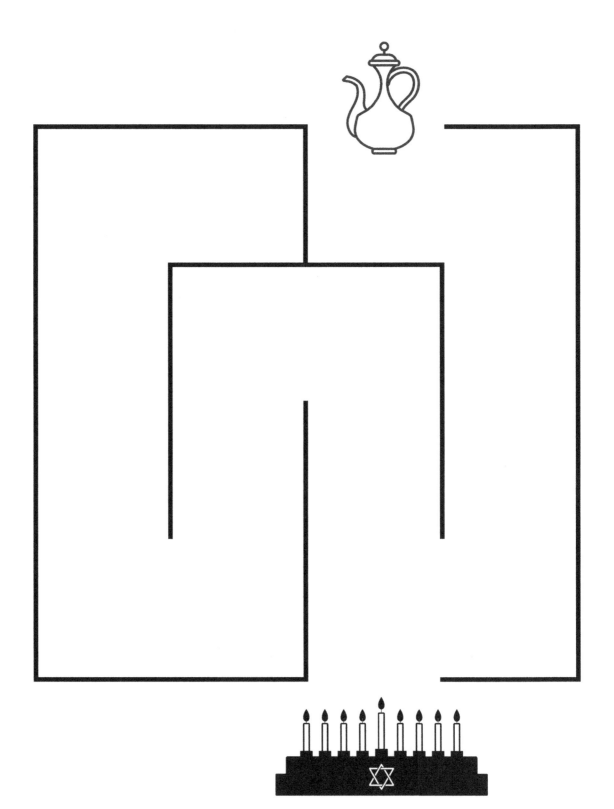

Word Search Circle The Below Words

Y	A	A	A	I	F	C	N	G
O	M	D	B	K	M	O	Y	A
X	Q	B	G	J	V	L	T	Z
V	A	I	I	E	M	E	X	X
R	A	S	M	M	V	A	X	I
U	R	B	M	E	E	D	E	R
T	E	Z	T	Y	I	D	N	T
R	O	X	V	F	G	Y	X	T
E	G	R	N	P	Z	K	O	A

Word List

november   rabbi   redeem   tevet

COUNT AND TRACE

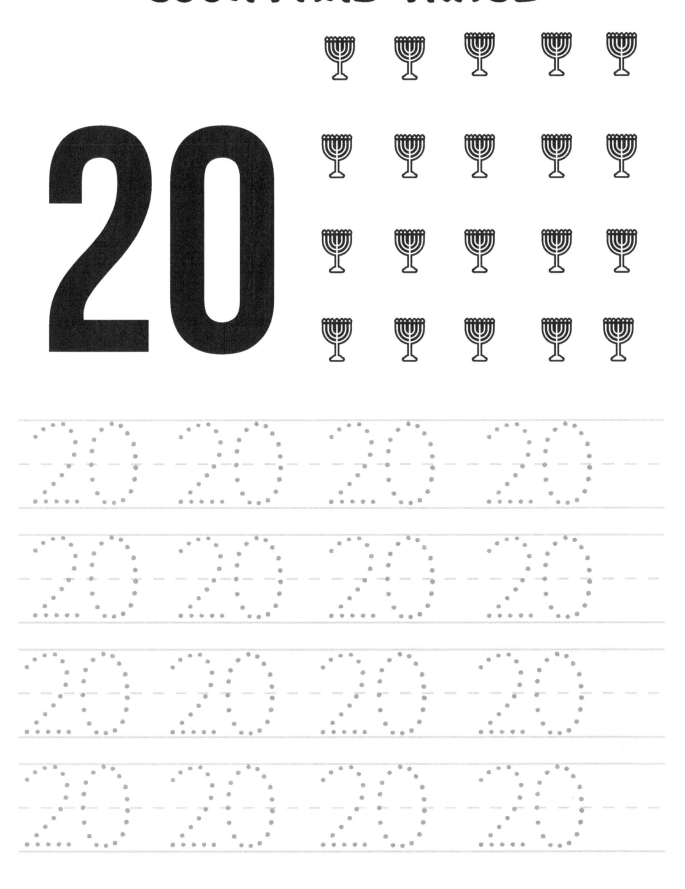

Spot The Differences

Count And Trace

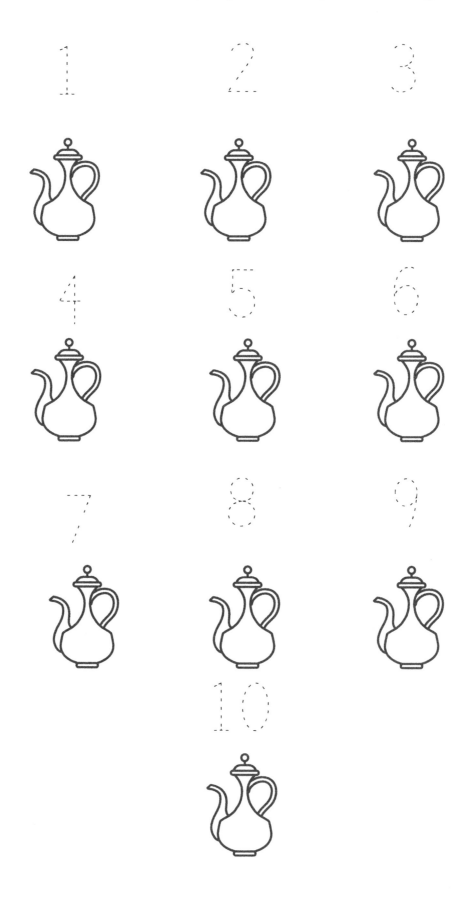

Word Search Circle The Below Words

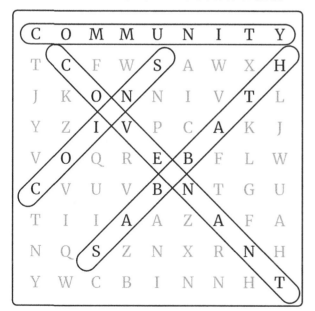

Word Search Circle The Below Words

Word Search Circle The Below Words

Word Search Circle The Below Words

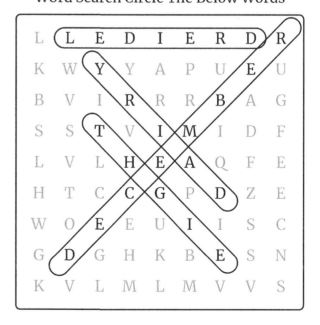

Word Search Circle The Below Words

```
N O J N R C T F L
I N C A M L B P F
Q R Y J J J S Q A
E V E N T H A H M
O M X L T Z T N I
W N H C K I G X L
S F A W A W K P Y
V N Q F Y C B W V
E S Z A K T I Q E
```

Word Search Circle The Below Words

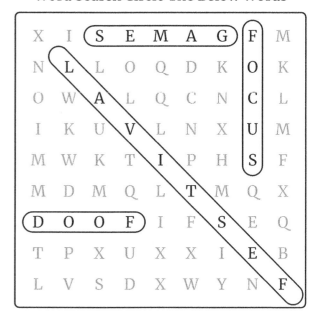

Word Search Circle The Below Words

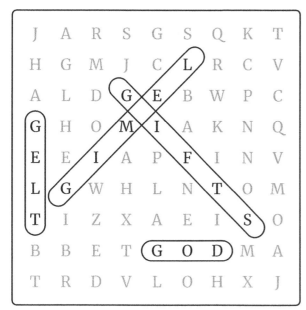

Word Search Circle The Below Words

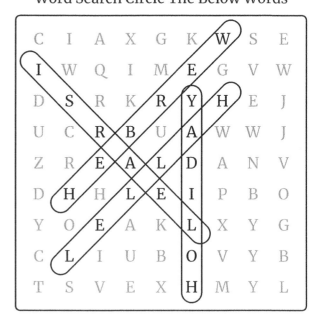

Word Search Circle The Below Words

H	P	W	L	K	Q	W	M	Z
X	J	E	W	I	S	H	V	L
L	V	R	U	N	O	S	D	P
Y	I	N	K	D	J	I	K	C
K	K	V	P	L	S	D	A	T
X	Q	V	I	E	H	L	F	J
J	H	Y	H	V	S	Q	F	X
M	Q	X	B	B	O	D	J	Z
V	E	L	S	I	K	T	M	I

Word Search Circle The Below Words

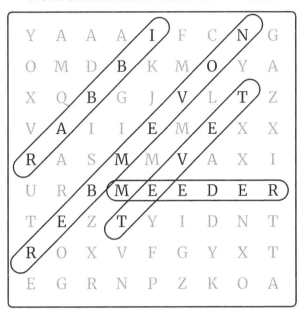

Y	A	A	A	I	F	C	N	G
O	M	D	B	K	M	O	Y	A
X	Q	B	G	J	V	L	T	Z
V	A	I	I	E	M	E	X	X
R	A	S	M	M	V	A	X	I
U	R	B	M	E	E	D	E	R
T	E	Z	T	Y	I	D	N	T
R	O	X	V	F	G	Y	X	T
E	G	R	N	P	Z	K	O	A

Help the menorah through the maze.

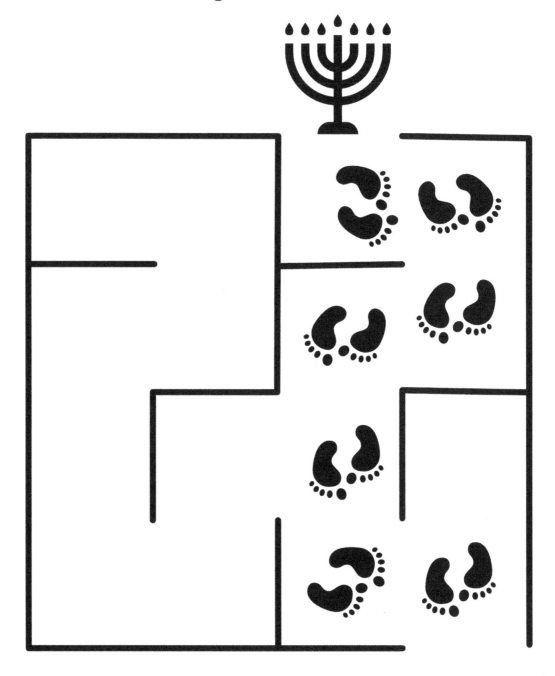

Help the book
through the maze.

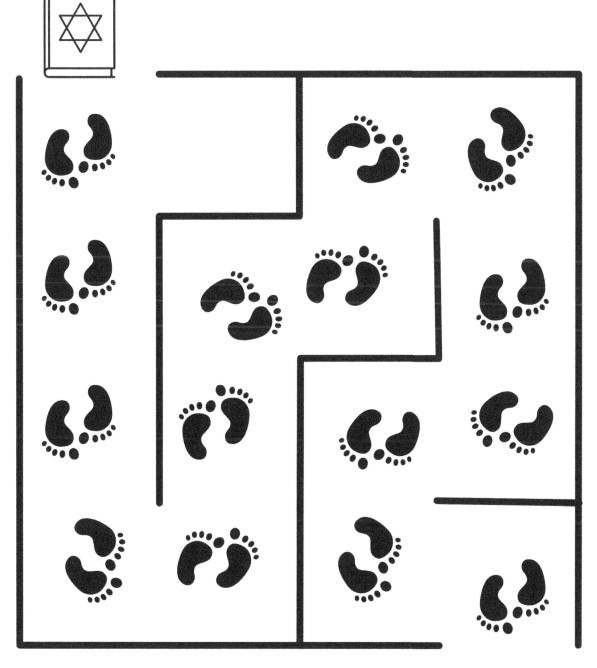

Help the present through the maze.

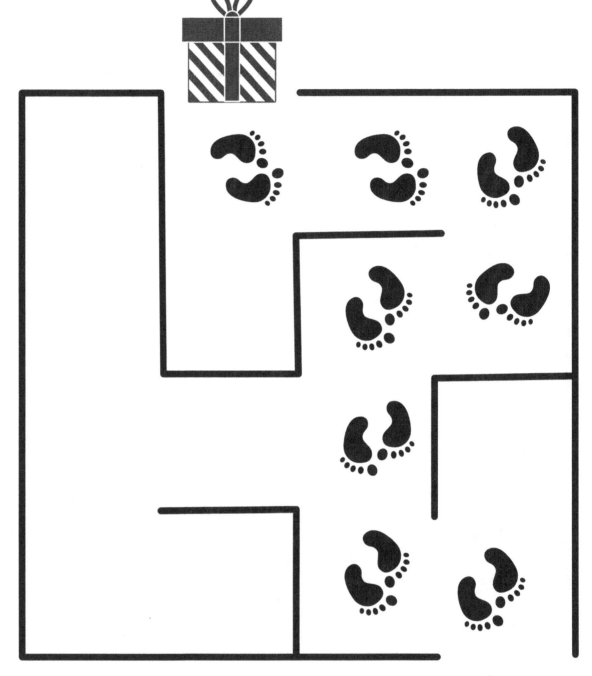

Help the cake through the maze.

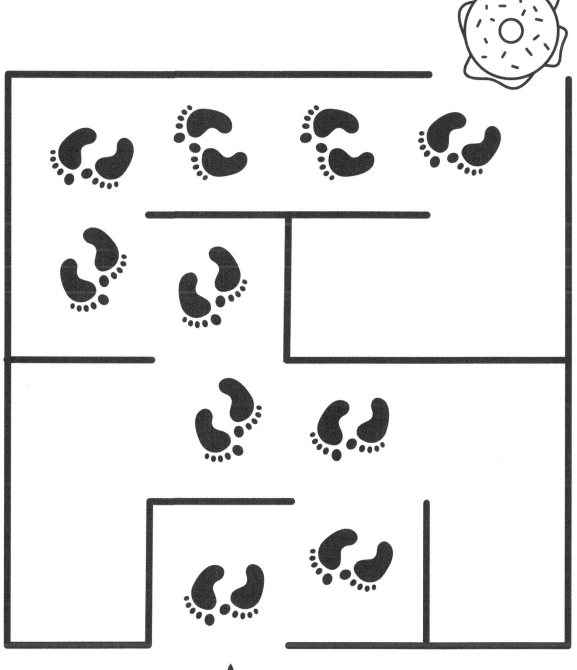

Help the star of david through the maze.

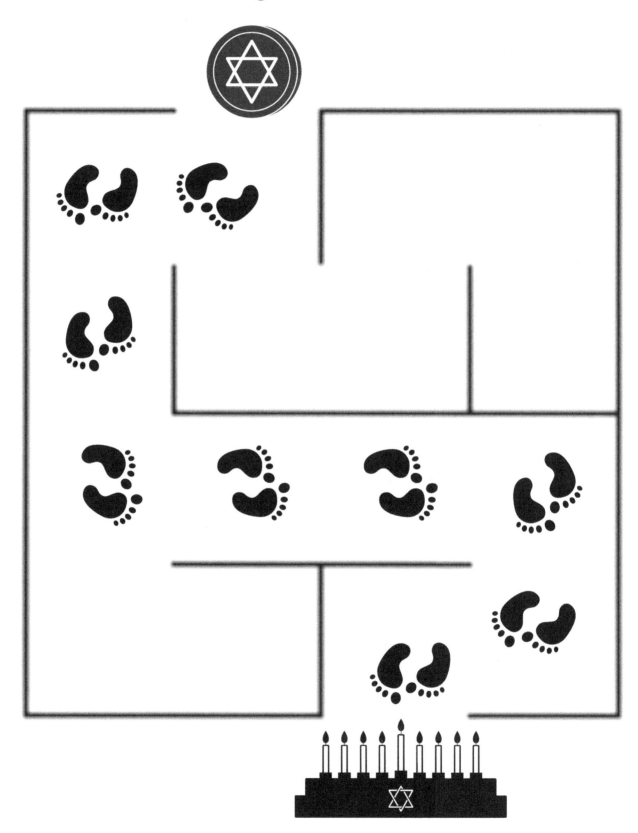

Help the cup through the maze.

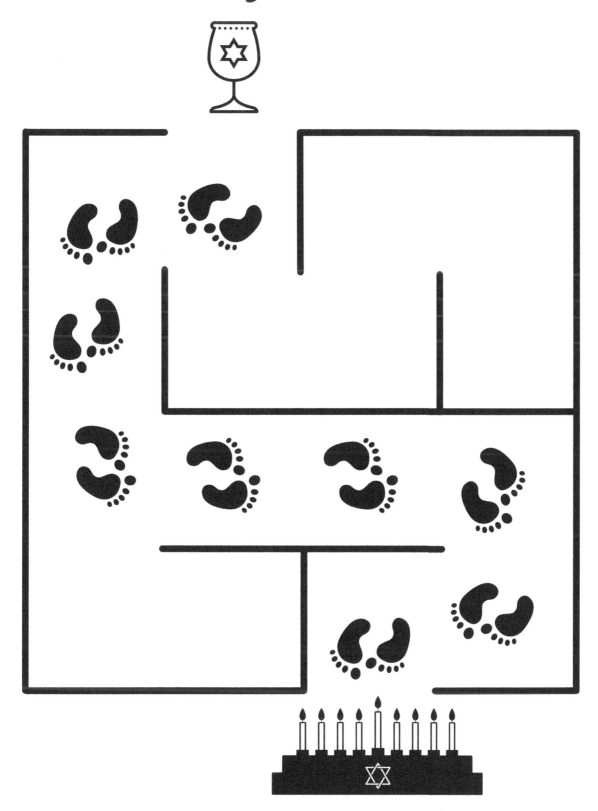

Help the candles through the maze.

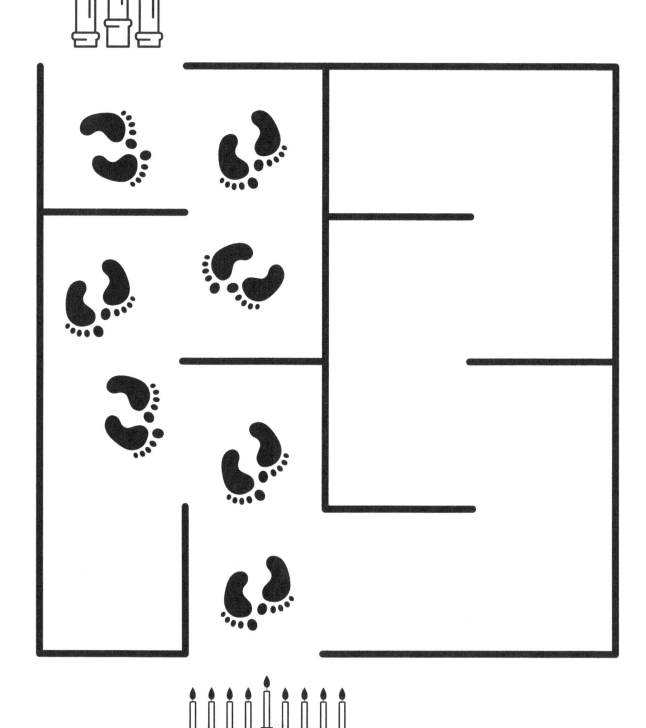

Help the dreidel through the maze.

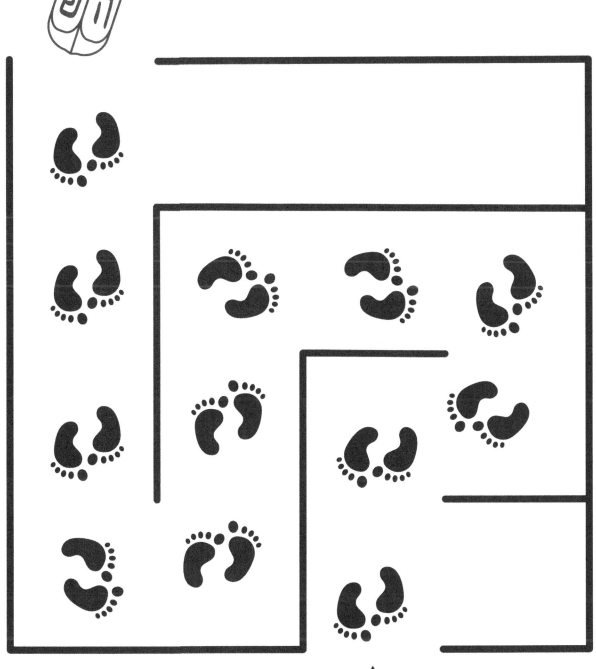

Help the gelt through the maze.

Help the ol through the maze.

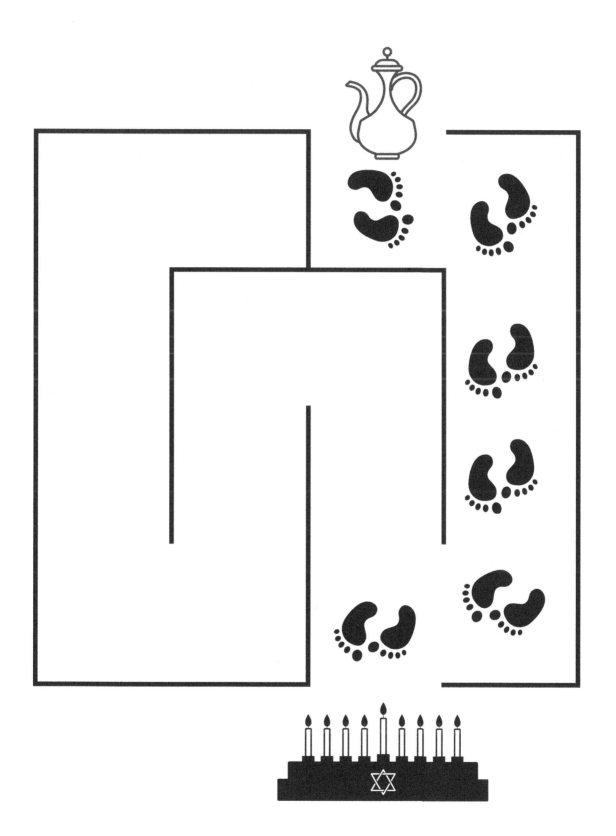

Spot The Differences

Spot The Differences

Spot The Difference

Spot The Difference

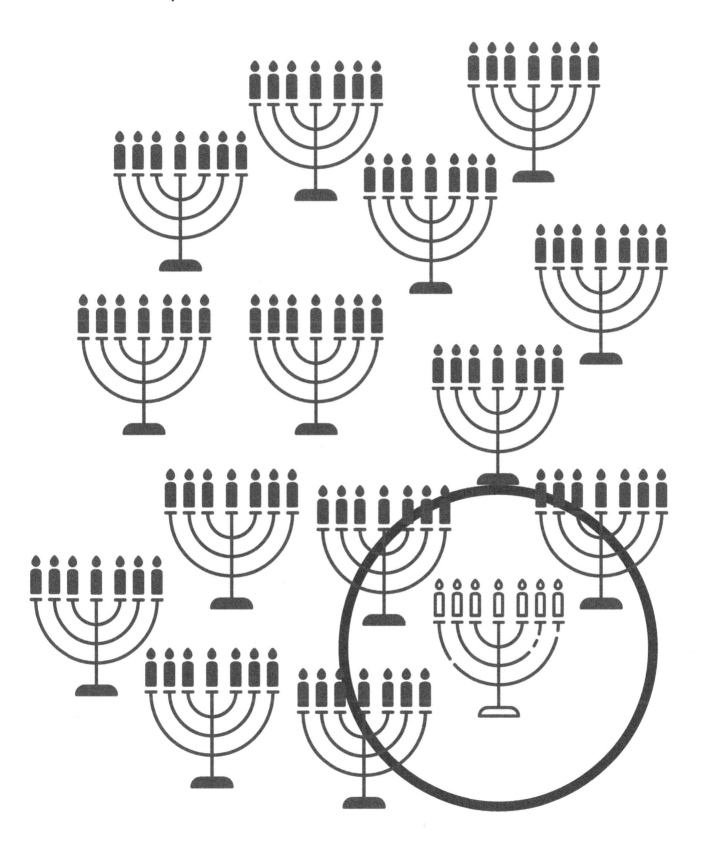

Spot The Difference

Spot The Difference

Spot The Difference

Spot The Difference

Spot The Differences

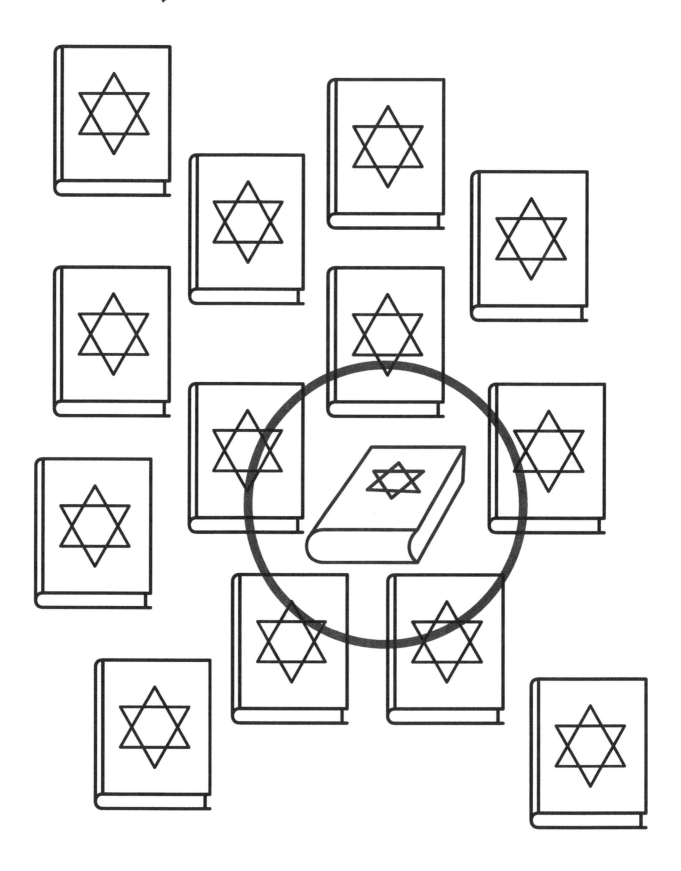

Spot The Differences

Made in the USA
Las Vegas, NV
18 December 2024

14704520R00052